You A

POSITIVE SOUL
BY JACQUELINE KADEMIAN

ISBN: 1722236078
ISBN-13: 978-1722236076

DEDICATION

This book is dedicated to all of the beautiful souls I have been blessed to work with. Time and time again, I am reminded just how important our confidence and self love is. I dedicate this book to you, a lovely soul who wants to improve her self love and confidence. I hope you learn in this process just how powerful you are. Always remember to love yourself.

JACQUELINE KADEMIAN

CONTENTS

Acknowledgments   i

Introduction   1

Day 1: Get Real &   6
Clear

Day 2: Letting Go   25
Of The Past

Day 3: Declutter   36

Day 4: Forgiving   43
Others

Day 5: Self   53
Forgiveness

Day 6: Clearing   62
Relationships

Day 7: Setting   72
Boundaries

Day 8: Monitor   83
Your Words

Day. 9: Love   90
Rampage

Day 10: Own Your   97
Strengths

Day 11: Accepting   105
Your Weaknesses

Day 12: Gratitude   114

Day 13: Self Care   122

Day 14: Step   132
Outside Your
Comfort Zone

Day 15: Finding   141
Your Passions

Day 16: Decision   148
Making

Day 17: Be You   154

Day 18: Act As If   162

Day 19: Kill The   167
Comparison Habit

Day 20: Give Back   177
to Others

Day 21: Reflect   183

About the Author   189

YOU ARE THAT GIRL

ACKNOWLEDGMENTS

I thank every single person who has given me the confidence and courage to be here today. To my loved ones, thank you for always loving me and teaching me what true confidence is. To my Positive Soul community, thank you for giving me the power to be of service to you. This is all thanks to you. Most importantly, I thank God for allowing me this opportunity and for always blessing me with more than I can thank Him for.

Introduction

Hello beautiful soul! I am so glad you have decided to purchase this book and get started on your journey towards confidence and self love.

My name is Jacqueline Kademian, and I am a Licensed Marriage & Family Therapist, Author and Entrepreneur. I am the creator of the personal development brand, Positive Soul. With over 7 years of experience providing professional therapy, online and in my own practice, I am reminded of just how crucial confidence is to a healthy and happy life.

I am so passionate about helping women like you transform their lives and learn to love themselves, from the inside out.

This book is so dear to my heart, for many reasons. As I just mentioned, I am so passionate about helping women develop their confidence. Time and time again through my work, I witness how integral confidence is to a happy life. As I will explain in the coming chapters, confidence and self love are crucial to your happiness and fulfillment in life.

Unfortunately, most of us have never been taught how to love ourselves. Our society makes it taboo to discuss such topics, as if having confidence is a bad thing. The word confidence and self love get thrown around as if it's dirty to have. Society equates confidence to being cocky nowadays. Having lost the meaning, it's my mission to help others understand the importance of having genuine self love and confidence.

Besides from helping you love yourself, this book is also meaningful to me because it highlights my experiences dealing with a lack of confidence, for most of my life.

Growing up, I struggled with insecurity for most of my life. Even up to a few years ago, I was insecure and unable to truly love myself. I thought I loved myself, but it was on a vain and inauthentic level.

In my earlier years growing up, I was mostly insecure about my weight. I was always a little chubbier than the rest of my peers in elementary and middle school. For most of my younger years, I would feel insecure about my weight and how I looked. I specifically remember how my insecurity led to shyness, introversion and hiding parts of my personality. Since I felt so insecure, I was very reserved. It was difficult for others to fully get to know me, as I always felt shy about who I really was. It was also difficult to get to know myself, as I often felt ashamed and embarrassed of my weight.

As I grew older, I eventually lost the weight. Finally, at the age of 16, I managed to get on track and shed the pounds I had on me for years. You could just imagine how happy I was, or so I thought! I finally felt good about my weight, and thought that weight loss would be the magic cure all. I felt "confident" in myself, due to how I looked, but I would soon find out that my confidence was inauthentic.

While the high of losing weight lasted a few years, I still did not feel fully confident deep down. At the time, I thought that I was confident because I looked good, but that couldn't be further from the truth. I thought that everything was great. I went about life, thinking that my insecurity issues were resolved. It wouldn't be until a few years later, after a specifically bad relationship, that I would realize that my insecurities were still there, looming and waiting to be brought up.

The year was 2014. At the time, I was in graduate school, feeling my best, and surrounded with great family and friends. I thought that I was the most confident I had ever been, certain that all of my insecurities were laid to rest. Well, as "confident" as I thought I was, I ended up attracting in a toxic and unhealthy relationship at that time. That relationship completely stripped me of any confidence I thought I had. The lack of love I had for myself led me to accept poor behavior. I became a shell of who I thought I was. I started to doubt myself and felt the worst I had ever felt. I felt unworthy and undeserving in life. I was a people pleaser and tried to make everyone feel comfortable, at my own expense.

All of my insecurities came out from before, stronger than ever. To my core, I became that insecure girl again, with a vengeance.

"What in the world happened? How could I be so insecure and steupid?" I often thought to myself. I was baffled. I couldn't believe I felt the way I did. I was truly confused to my core. I thought that my

insecurities from the past were all taken care of and healed. *So how did I attract in this relationship? How did I let myself be treated in such a way?* That was when it all made sense.

I finally had my moment of realization. I finally realized that confidence had nothing to do with how I looked or how much weight I lost. I realized that confidence came from the inside out, not the other way around.

I made the common mistake of thinking that since I felt great physically, I felt great emotionally as well. I thought that with the weight loss, all of my emotional struggles were over. I never realized how deep my insecurity went. I didn't understand that I had to heal my emotional wounds in order to be truly confident.

Weight loss didn't help my confidence, it just masked my insecurities. I finally learned that confidence isn't about being pretty, having the best body, making money, having a nice car and so forth.

Confidence doesn't come from jumping from relationship to relationship. Confidence is a result of how you feel about yourself on the inside. That was the lesson that I learned, that I am so passionate about teaching you in this book.

I find that many women who come to me feel the same way I felt years ago. They are confused and baffled that they feel the way they do. All of them are successful, kind, good-hearted and beautiful women. Yet, they feel insecure and can't seem to love themselves.

I was able to fully heal and love myself from the inside out, so I fully understand what it takes to develop true confidence. Now, no matter what I look like or what my life is, I have authentic confidence from the inside out. I can truly say that I love myself. I feel confident in who I am, and I am so proud of all the work I have accomplished.

True confidence makes you indestructible. It doesn't matter what anyone else thinks or says about you; if you have true confidence in yourself, the sky is the limit. Confidence is the ultimate quality you can possess, which is why teaching you this material is so dear to my heart.

The techniques and tools that I have used to develop authentic confidence are detailed in this book. Going through my own struggles with confidence, I feel confident that this guidebook will help you. Confidence is a habit that you can master. Just like the athlete gets better at his sport by practicing daily, you will grow your confidence by practicing it daily.

So, without further ado, I am so excited to present with you this book. **I want you to get acquainted with the new you, the new girl that you will be after this experience.**

Being THAT girl is all about being the most confident, empowered & assured version of yourself. Prepare to be the version of yourself who feels the best & knows her value, from the inside out. Prepare to feel confident on the inside, and not just the outside.

Being that girl is about progress, not perfection. As you go through this book, I want you to remember that this is a journey. It will take some time for you to get used to the different tasks and activities.

As mentioned, **confidence is a habit;** it's like a muscle that will get stronger the more you use it. When going through this 21 day journey, remember that practice will make perfection. Much of this material is meant to be practiced and implemented in your life daily. The more you can use these skills, the more you will grow your confidence.

What is Confidence?

The word confidence seems to be thrown around everywhere these days. I mean what does it really mean? Does anyone know?

To describe what confidence means, I first want to discuss what it doesn't mean. Confidence is not being arrogant. Confidence is not cockiness. Confidence is definitely not Narcissism (this word seems to be thrown around everywhere these days). Confidence is not vanity and it definitely doesn't mean that you are full of yourself. Confidence is not a negative concept. Confidence is actually the purest vibration one can be omitting into the world.

Confidence is to have regard for your own well being and happiness, even in the midst of having flaws. To be confident, you must make your wellbeing your priority. You view yourself as valuable. You prioritize yourself. Flaws and all, you love yourself for being who you are. You also realize that in order to offer anything to others, you must first be taking care of yourself.

Confidence is the ultimate act of selflessness. When you love yourself, you know how to love others. We all come with flaws and imperfections. When you accept and love your own flaws, you can also love the flaws in others.

When you make your wellbeing a priority, you are communicating to the Universe that you are important and worthy. From that high vibe place, you attract similar experiences and people. The more confident you are, the more likely you will attract confident people into your life.

I want you to view your act of being confident as a gift to the world. When you learn how to genuinely love yourself, you have so much to offer. You will help uplift others and inspire them to do the same. You will naturally attract so much abundance into your life. You will find that you will manifest your desires with ease. You will be confident no matter what happens. Your confidence will be a pure gift to the world.

Love is the most pure vibration we can be offering to the Universe. Once you direct that love within, love will fill you in profound ways.

Why 21 Days?

When choosing the length of this book, I was presented with different lengths. I was originally going to make this into a 30 day guidebook, but then I realized that 30 days may seem too long and daunting. I decided on the 21 day length for many reasons.

The 21 day model is short term, present-focused and very doable. When starting a new habit, I believe it's very important to set yourself up for success. The 21 day model allows you to do that, as you will have ample opportunity to integrate this new habit of confidence. 21 days is a great starting point for integrating a new habit into your life.

When it comes to the psychology of the mind, short term goals are just as important as long term goals. As you complete this guide, psychologically you will be priming yourself for success.

You see, the more you experience success with this guide, the more motivation you will have to continue these habits. So, if you can complete this 21 day guide, you will have more motivation to apply these principles long after the book is over. Human psychology is amazing right?

21 days will set you up for success, especially in the confidence department. Once you apply these skills, you will find that with practice, they will become second nature.

How does this work?

This workbook is meant to be used over a period of 21 days. It is best used when you take it one day at a time. Each day, there will be a new skill or exercise I will go over. You will also be asked to journal each day, reflecting upon the lesson of the day.

By using this workbook over a 21 day period, you will be able to practice each skill and begin to implement it into your daily life. After 21 days of going through this book, feel free to start the process again. You can then feel more free when it comes to implementing the techniques and adding it to your daily routine.

Be as honest and vulnerable as you can be. This is your book, and a space where you can be authentically you. The more honest you are, the more progress you will make. Keep this as a sacred space for yourself.

Have fun with this book and remember that developing confidence is a beautiful process. You will feel many emotions as you go through this book, so don't be shocked if you do. Be kind and loving to yourself.

I hope you are able to practice each of these skills and continue applying them after the 21 days are up. Here is to you becoming THAT girl and the best version of yourself ever.

Day 1:

Get Real + Clear

Welcome to day 1! I am so excited to begin this 21 day journey with you. Day 1 is all about getting real and clear about where you are right now and where you want to be after this 21 day journey.

In order for you to move forward and develop your confidence, you first need to get real about your current confidence status. What often holds us back is failing to acknowledge where we currently are.

If you are here, I am sure that you are struggling with insecurity or a lack of confidence in your life. You may be struggling with feelings of unworthiness. You may find yourself self sabotaging in life. You may have a difficult time accepting love and being open to relationships. You may put yourself down and feel unworthy of happiness in life. Whatever the case is, I want you to reflect about where you are right now on your confidence journey, in the most honest way possible.

It's important to note that the first step in making any change comes with acknowledgment. In therapy, often the most difficult aspect of treatment is getting clients' to acknowledge that they are struggling. We have been taught that it's weak to talk about our problems and that if we deny them they will go away. That is clearly not the case!

Today, you are going to be asked to reflect upon your specific confidence struggles. Be as honest and vulnerable as you can be. Remember that denial is the enemy of success. You can't make any positive changes if you deny what is really happening.

So many of us have been taught that denial is the way to go. We learn to sweep things under the rug, to ignore problems, to not discuss what's going wrong. This is toxic to our health. Ignoring what's really happening affects you more than you think it would.

So, step 1 in developing confidence comes with an honest appraisal of where you are today. I want you to be the most confident and loving version of yourself there is. I want you to be happy and full of life. In order to get there, it's crucial for you to admit the struggles you are having right now. In order to grow, you must get clear about everything that is holding you back.

For today, I want you to really focus on the areas of your life where you are lacking in confidence. I want you to be honest with yourself and let it all out.

This is your private workbook and I want you to feel safe in expressing yourself. The more you let it all out, the more transformational work we can do with one another.

Day 1 Reflection

What do you feel the most insecure about? Write
out all of your insecure thoughts.

How do your insecurities create problems in your
life? Write about all the different ways your
insecurities manifest.
*Ex: Feeling unworthy may make you not want to date
anyone.*

What aspects of your life is a lack of confidence affecting the most?
Ex: relationships, career, friends, school, etc

How long have you been feeling this way? Were there any major events in your life that made you feel insecure?

How may you have picked up on your insecurities
from others?
Ex: family, friends, past relationships, past experiences

What is your motivation for improving your
confidence and self love?

Yay! You got through the questions. I am so proud of you. I know how difficult it can be to answer those questions from an honest and vulnerable place.

Now that you have reflected upon your current state, I want to shift gears a bit. Everything you wrote down is extremely meaningful and important, however we are not going to focus on them. That is just the baseline for how you are feeling right now.

To track how much you have improved in the confidence department, we make a note of your baseline. However, we don't focus on your baseline. Your baseline will serve itself on the few pages you just wrote on. That's it. From here on out, we will focus on the positives and how you can improve your confidence.

We got real, now let's get CLEAR. If the above exercise made you feel negative in anyway, I recommend taking a break at this point and coming back to this portion later today. It's important for this next part that you are in a good feeling state.

Now that you know how a lack of confidence has impacted your life, I want you to get clear about the confidence goals you have for this 21 day journey. These will be your short term goals.

Setting goals is an extremely important process in all aspects of your life. You need to be clear and specific with what your goals are.

Your goals do not have to be big and grand, as 21 days is just the start to completing your long term goals. I want you to think about some short term goals you can envision yourself accomplishing after going through this 21 day journey.

Remember, it's all about the process. I will provide you with some examples of goals below.

Example Goals:

1. I am taking part in self care activities throughout the week.
2. I am learning how to speak positively about myself.
3. I am in the process of setting boundaries and saying "No" to others.
4. I am not using derogatory terms to refer to myself, such as fat, ugly, etc.
5. I am not taking the behavior of others personally.
6. I am not comparing myself to others.

7. I am completing a course/hobby/activity that speaks to my spirit.
8. I am feeling better and my mood is improved.
9. I am trying new things and putting myself out there.
10. I am speaking up for myself.

Now, it's your turn! On the next page, I want you to create a list of short term goals for this 21 day process. Don't feel any pressure to create a certain amount of goals. Just put down as many as you feel called to do so.

Short Term Goals

1.

2.

3.

4.

5.

6.

7.

8.

9.

10.

.

Overall, how do you want to feel after this 21 day journey?

How will you know that you are more confident?

Are you ready to commit to this program and consistently go through the 21 days?

Day 2: Letting go of the past

Welcome to Day 2! Day 1 was a difficult one, as it pushed you to get real and clear about where you are right now, and where you want to be in the confidence department.

Getting real and clear is crucial in all aspects of your life. When faced with any new challenge you are working towards, make sure that the first step entails taking an inventory of where you are and where you want to be.

Now that you are aware of your baseline and your goals for this 21 day process, I want to get into the core work! YAY! For Day 2, the focus is going to be your past, so you can release it and work from the present moment.

What does your past have to do with your confidence? In short, it has everything to do with your self love and confidence. When we hold onto anything from the past, we are holding onto stagnant energy that is blocking the flow of confidence into our lives.

A lot of our current negative beliefs are based on our past and what's happened throughout our lives. We hold onto past events, thoughts, and situations that are harmful for us. We relive unfortunate moments. We hold onto specific memories that don't serve us. The truth is, you are not powerless to your past. You have the power to release the past and focus on the present moment.

I am a huge believer of energy. I really believe that the energy we carry impacts every aspect of our lives. When you hold onto bitterness, resentment, anger and frustration, you block the energy of love.

Having self love can't come into your experience if you are carrying onto anything from the past.

This is not to say that you shouldn't feel the way you do. You are entitled to feel ANY emotion that you feel. However, holding onto negative energy only harms you in the long run. It affects your mental and physical health. It keeps you living in the past, where you are unable to focus on the present.

What does it mean to let go of the past? I mean, if you let go, does that mean that you are forgetting about what happened? Does that mean that you are accepting the past?

These are common fears that we all have. We think that if we let go of something, we are forgetting about it or accepting it in our lives. I'm here to remind you that letting go of the past does not mean that you are accepting of it, forgetting it or even forgiving it.

Letting go means that you no longer choose to allow the past to control you. You detach from the past affecting your life. You acknowledge the past, but you let go of having it rule your life.

Your past no longer clouds your mind and stays at the forefront of all of your thoughts. You acknowledge the past and choose to focus on the present instead. The present is where all of your power lies. When you find yourself overly focusing on the past, you are losing out on your life now.

Focusing on the present is a choice. It means that you recognize the importance of detaching from the past and moving forward.

Do you want to develop your self love and confidence massively? Are you ready for this new chapter in your life? It's time to detach from the past and move forward.

One of the main reasons you are struggling right now with self love/confidence is because you are stuck in the past. No matter what is affecting your confidence, there is a root to it that lies in your past. It can be uncomfortable to go there and to realize how much power your past still has over you.

There is also another portion to this, which will help you understand why you may be giving your past so much power. You see love, sometimes it feels safer to remain in the past, in an insecure state that you are in. This has everything to do with your comfort zone.

Your comfort zone at this point is having insecurities, doubts and limitations. Yes, it sounds crazy, but it's true! You see, you already know what it feels like to feel this way. You are used to the negative thoughts in your head. It feels safe and comfortable.

Your comfort zone keeps you safe. No matter what happens, you already know what it's like to feel insecure, so there are no unknown elements that can throw you off. It's much scarier to have confidence and self love. It's the unknown. You don't know what to expect.

It's time we take the bandaid off and create a new comfort zone, one filled with confidence and love.

Today, I want you to take the time and really think about what you are holding onto from the past that is affecting your confidence. It can be an experience you went through. It can be comments others have made that made you doubt yourself. It can be a failed business or relationship you are holding onto. It can be a mistake you made that you are beating yourself up over. It can be what you heard from your parents about your abilities. Whatever it is, I want you to bring it to light, so we can release it.

Today is a difficult day of cleansing and growth. However, in order to develop self love, you must be willing to do the difficult work. Releasing the past is one of the most transformational tools you can do to increase your confidence.

It truly helped me recognize what was holding me back and what I had to do to develop true confidence.

I am very proud of you for taking the time today to release your past. I know how difficult it can be. I want you to know that the past can set you free. Your power lies in the present and you are one step closer to self love.

Day 2 Reflection

What specific negative thoughts, beliefs, feelings, events are you holding onto from the past that can be affecting your confidence? Use this page to write down anything that you need to release from the past.

Ex: I am holding onto negative comments my ex boyfriend said about me. I think that I am unworthy and undeserving of love. I am holding onto my friend abandoning me.

It's time to release the above. On the lines below, I want you to CHOOSE to let go of what you wrote above.

Ex: Today, I choose to let go of…the bad names my ex boyfriend called me during our relationship.

Today, I choose to let go of…

Today, I choose to let go of…

Today, I choose to let go of…

Today, I choose to let go of…

Today, I choose to let go of…

Today, I choose to let go of...

Today, I choose to let go of...

Today, I choose to let go of...

Today, I choose to let go of...

Today, I choose to let go of...

What feelings are coming up as you complete these exercises? Release all of the negative feelings you are experiencing.

Today, I release these feelings...

List the positive feelings you are inviting into your life.

Repeat and write down this affirmation, add anything else that resonates with you;

"Today, I choose to release the past. I recognize that the past happened and I fully acknowledge it. I decide to let go of all the negative feelings, thoughts and beliefs that are holding me back. I choose to let go for my own self, not anyone else. The past no longer has power over me. I have power over my life. I am strong and fearless. I am beginning to be filled with love and confidence in myself. By releasing the past, I invite confidence and love in. "

Day 3: Declutter

Welcome to Day 3!

Day 3's focus may confuse you a bit, but decluttering is so important when it comes to developing your confidence and self love.

You may be wondering, "What in the world does decluttering have to do with confidence?!". I'm here to tell you that it has everything to do with your confidence. In fact, clutter impacts every aspect of your life.

Having a bunch of "stuff" is a huge drain to your energy. When you hold onto so many things, you are blocking new energy from coming into your life. Physical objects have energy, every single one of them. You may think that your stuff are tucked away in closets, but they each contain their own unique energy. The more clutter you have, the more you are taking the space of new, vibrant energy to come in.

Keeping your energy field open and clean will tremendously increase your self love and confidence. There is no better place to start that energy clean-up than at home, at your office, or in your car. Wherever it is that you frequent daily, it's time to declutter and open up space for new energy to flow into your life.

Once you clean and declutter your environment, you will feel so much lighter. In fact, there have been hundreds of research studies that show how detrimental clutter can be to your mental and physical health.

Clutter can lead to more stress, decreased happiness, increased procrastination, less productive mental energy and so much more. It's no secret that clutter can have major effects on your life.

In the confidence department, you are ready to invite new, positive energy into your life. But did you know that decluttering can also improve other aspects of your life? Whether you want to manifest love, money, happiness, friendships & on, you need to have room to invite that energy in. Stagnant energy serves as a block to abundance, in all aspects of your life.

So, today's challenge will help you clear up energy in all aspects of your life. Actually, when you work on your confidence, you will find that all aspects of your life will improve (more on that later).

For example, imagine if you are trying to manifest love, but you have a bunch of old love cards from your ex who broke your heart. Those old cards may seem harmless to you, but in actuality they are keeping the energy of that relationship alive in your life. If you want new love, you need to make space to invite that in. It's difficult to do that if you still are keeping your ex alive energetically in your home.

Now apply this concept to any area of your life. When we are feeling insecure and down on ourselves, we often have a bunch of stuff that reminds us of those times. That stuff is not serving us. The clutter is just a reminder of old energy that is hanging over our heads.

Getting rid of clutter feels so liberating! I remember when I first heard about this concept, I thought it was silly and ridiculous. I put it off for a few days at first. I kept thinking that since my clutter was out of sight, it wouldn't affect me. Well, I was wrong!

I decided to declutter after putting it off for weeks, and it was beyond therapeutic. I remember how good it felt to get rid of my old belongings. The feeling has become addicting. Energetically, I feel so free and great every time I declutter. Now, I set up a monthly decluttering session. I notice myself becoming more clear, creative and focused after every cleaning session.

For today, I want you to commit to decluttering an aspect of your space where you spend the most time in. This can be your room, kitchen, closet, car, work space & on. If you are short on time today, you can start the decluttering and then come back to it. You don't have to stay up until 3 am decluttering, but make sure you commit to getting started.

If you have more time in the next few days or after the challenge ends, I recommend decluttering as many places as you can.

If you want to further raise your vibration and make the most of this process, use this as an opportunity to act as if you are already the most confident version of yourself. Think of yourself from that space, how would the most confident version of yourself keep her room? Her workplace? Her car?

As you declutter, ask yourself, "Would I keep this around if I was confident? How would this area look if I was the most confident me?".

Think of yourself as the confident girl you know you are and declutter from that space. This often makes the process more fun and easy to complete.

After you declutter, create a plan of action for what you will do with your stuff. You can decide to donate it, give it to someone, have a garage sale and so forth. Whatever it is you do with it, realize that you will be helping someone else feel better as they receive your stuff.

The Universe is all about an exchange of energy. When you do good for someone and bless them with your belongings, you will receive good back. Donating your belongings, making someone else's day will only make you feel more confident about yourself.

Day 3 Reflection

Set an area you want to declutter and commit to when you will do it today. After you declutter, come back and answer the remaining questions.

How did it feel for you to declutter?

What old feelings and thoughts did you release with your belongings?

Were you able to feel a release of energy as you decluttered?

What new energy are you now inviting into your life?

What will you do with the clutter? Make a plan of action.

Day 4:

Forgiving Others

Now that you have decluttered your physical space, I am sure you are feeling the positive effects already! I'm so proud of you for making it to Day 4 of this journey.

Yesterday, we dealt with your physical stuff. Today, we are going to address the emotional aspects of decluttering.

Today's lesson may be more emotional than others, but remember that developing your self love is difficult work at times. Today we will be going over the main task of decluttering your emotional baggage; the task of forgiveness and acceptance of the past.

If you are struggling with confidence, there is an emotional root to it. Our confidence is highly based on our emotions. We develop insecurity and a lack of confidence due to negative emotions we have felt. Today, we are going to focus on releasing and clearing any emotional ties you may have that lead to insecurity.

What is emotional baggage? Emotional baggage refers to the limiting beliefs, insecurities, past experiences, societal messages and doubts that are holding you back. It can be due to your childhood, what you were taught to believe, how others made you feel, past relationships, past situations and so forth.

Your emotional landscape is vast and complex. Most of our emotional baggage stems from years and decades ago. We learn to stuff down our negative emotions and deny that they exist. This leads to repression of our emotions, which can manifest in insecurity, self doubt, negative feelings about oneself and so forth.

When we don't clear out our emotional ties, we become literally and figuratively stuck. I'm sure you have noticed how debilitating it is to have a lack of confidence. Insecurity stops you from fully living your life and enjoying what life has to offer. It makes you scared. It keeps you in your comfort zone of fear. It leads into self doubt and fear. It keeps you stuck in the same place, year after year.

As they say, a comfort zone is a terrible place to be! It's better to put yourself out there and fail, then to stay stagnant in a comfort zone. However, when you don't take the time to address what's going on emotionally, your ego will convince you to stay in your comfort zone. This exercise today is meant to help you clear your emotions, so that you can take the next leap and fully live your life.

The biggest step in clearing emotional baggage comes with forgiveness. Forgiveness is the act of letting go and releasing past transgressions. We need to forgive others, which we will do today, and we need to forgive ourselves, which is for tomorrow.

I am sure that others have wronged you in some way on your time on Earth. Some people are able to forgive easily and let it go. For others, it's more difficult, which is understandable. For people who have been bullied or harassed by others, it can be difficult to look to the bully and forgive. *I mean, why do we have to forgive? Is it really necessary for developing confidence?*

Short answer, yes it is.

You have to forgive because holding onto anger only affects you. That's right, it doesn't affect anyone else but you. Your anger is poison to your soul. By holding onto anger and resentment, you are blocking so much abundance from coming your way.

It may seem unfair that you have to forgive someone who caused you so much harm, but remember, this isn't about them. This is always about you. You are forgiving others for yourself. Let those that harm others keep staying miserable and stagnant, because I promise you that they are. Have you ever met a bully doing good? I bet you haven't.

To grow and develop your confidence, you have to forgive others and make peace with releasing the pain.

I want you to understand that forgiveness does not mean that you accept or condone what happened to you. Forgiveness is not acceptance of bad behavior. Forgiveness does not mean that you "lost". Forgiveness does not mean that you have to accept similar behavior in the future.

Forgiveness is a release of negative energy, so that you can move on.

Forgiveness helps you move on and live your life. When you are able to forgive others, you commit an act of love towards yourself. You finally decide that you are no longer going to focus on the past. You are all about the present moment, which is where your power lies.

Take the first step into owning your power today, by practicing forgiveness of others.

Is there anyone you need to forgive? Any lingering negative feelings towards someone? Think about them and work on forgiving them today through the exercises.

I know how difficult this day can be. It was difficult for me to forgive an ex who was very manipulative and treated me badly, however when I did I felt so much better. I finally felt that I wasn't affected by him anymore. By forgiving him, I released him from my energy. He no longer takes up mental space for me. By forgiving him, I opened up doors for another amazing relationship to come into my life.

Below, complete the forgiveness list. Complete the prompt as many times as you need to. Be as detailed as you can about what you are forgiving each person for. Take your time. Remember that this is about you forgiving others. Don't add yourself to the mix just yet.

Forgiveness List

Today, I choose to forgive _____ for _____...

Today, I choose to forgive _____ for _____...

Today, I choose to forgive _____ for _____...

Today, I choose to forgive _____ for _____ ...

Today, I choose to forgive _____ for _____ ...

Today, I choose to forgive _____ for _____ ...

Today, I choose to forgive _____ for _____ ...

Today, I choose to forgive _____ for _____ ...

Today, I choose to forgive _____ for _____...

Today, I choose to forgive _____ for _____...

Today, I choose to forgive _____ for _____...

Today, I choose to forgive _____ for _____...

How did it feel for you to forgive? What emotions came up for you?

Below, release all of the negative emotions that you felt during the exercise.

Today, I release these feelings...

Do you feel more in control of your life now that you no longer choose to allow the past to control you?

Day 5:

Self Forgiveness

Day 4 was a difficult one. It can be so difficult to forgive others from the past. I hope you feel proud of yourself for taking the first steps in healing and releasing the past from having anymore control over your life.

As difficult as forgiveness is, it's extremely healing. It's so rewarding when you finally release those old feelings you've been harboring for years. I remember how great I felt when I forgave others in my life. I truly felt like a new woman.

By practicing forgiveness, you are practicing an act of self love. A truly confident person is able to forgive and move on in life. This is truly an act of love towards yourself, as you are showing yourself that your present is more important than your past.

Yesterday, you began to clear your heart by forgiving others. You remembered a lot of what you had stuffed down. You became vulnerable and let it all out. The act of releasing your thoughts and feelings will help you develop your confidence, as you learn how to become more comfortable with yourself.

For today, I want you to continue decluttering your emotional baggage, by forgiving yourself. We often don't realize how much of our insecurity is self inflicted. We are very hard on ourselves. We over judge ourselves and set up strict standards that we need to follow.

Have you ever done this? Judged yourself or put yourself down several times because of a mistake you made? What about feeling badly about something you did even years after it passed?

I know this feeling all too well. I am sure you do too. It's so unfortunate how judgmental and vindictive we can be to our own selves.

Instead of loving ourselves, flaws and all, we hold ourselves to a higher standard than others. We are our harshest critics and this leads to self doubt, insecurity, and confidence issues.

The truth is, you will make mistakes in life. You will disappoint yourself. You will disappoint others. You will look back and wonder how you did certain things. You will feel badly about certain actions or certain thoughts you had. You will regret some decisions you made.

This doesn't make you any less lovable or worthy of anything. You are human! Just like the rest of us, this will happen to you. Instead of fighting it, make peace with the fact that you are a human, and mistakes will happen sometimes.

Instead of beating yourself up for your mistakes, choose to grow and learn from them. If you are learning from your mistakes, you are growing and becoming a better version of yourself. True confidence comes in recognizing this and aiming to be the best version of yourself. This doesn't mean that you won't make mistakes in your life, you probably will again, but you will use it as an opportunity to grow.

I still make mistakes in life and have moments of disappointment, but they are far less now that I am less critical of myself. I don't judge myself heavily or feel guilty for months after something goes wrong. I forgive myself and strive to be better. This is what I wish for you as well with this daily lesson.

Today, the focus is on forgiving yourself. If you are struggling with self confidence issues, I know for a fact that there is something in your life that you feel badly about. Whatever it is, just know that holding onto it and feeling bad about it does nothing for you. Holding onto the past builds up that negative and stagnant energy I want you to escape from.

I know so many people who don't want to forgive themselves. They feel guilty for having self love. They feel guilty for being happy. They think that the only way to get "payback" on themselves is to relive the pain. Let's stop this negative cycle today. It's self sabotaging and it does nothing for you.

We want to constantly suffer and suffer and suffer. Maybe if we suffer enough, we will feel better about the past. No amount of "suffering" will ever make you feel good about yourself.

Those feelings of guilt are your insecurities and limits trying to run the show. It's your ego peeking it's head out. Your ego wants you to stay small. It wants you to be in your comfort zone of negative feelings. Decide today that you are the architect of your life, not your ego.

Whatever has happened in the past, it's time to accept it, release it and then move on. Forgiveness will help you do just that.

As you forgive yourself, you release negative energetic ties that have been weighing you down for years. Once you break up with that energy, you make room for positive energy to come into your life. You are not the past and the mistakes you have made. You are so much more than that.

Choose today to be the day that you break up with your past. This exercise alone will help you feel lighter and more at peace. You will start to feel more grounded. You will start to feel love for yourself, as you realize that you are human and make mistakes. Self forgiveness is the ultimate act of showing love to yourself.

Remember, the most important question is, are you growing and learning from the mistakes? That's what matters.

Below, I want you to complete a forgiveness list for yourself. Be as detailed as you can about what you are forgiving for. Repeat this exercise as many times as you need to.

Forgiveness List

Today, I choose to forgive myself for…

Today, I choose to forgive myself for…

Today, I choose to forgive myself for…

Today, I choose to forgive myself for…

Today, I choose to forgive myself for…

Today, I choose to forgive myself for...

Today, I choose to forgive myself for...

Today, I choose to forgive myself for...

Today, I choose to forgive myself for...

Today, I choose to forgive myself for...

Today, I choose to forgive myself for...

How does it feel to forgive yourself and release your emotions?

Below, release all of the negative emotions that you felt during the exercise.

Today, I release these feelings...

Day 6: Clearing Relationships

Welcome to Day 6! You are almost a week in the challenge. I hope you are already feeling the love you are pouring inside of you, simply by releasing and letting go of the past.

This first week has been difficult work! Your work is not going unnoticed and it is setting you up for success. If you feel lighter and more in control of your life, you are doing amazing so far and are on your way towards confidence and self love.

This is the work that will set you up for success in the coming weeks.

For Day 6, we will continue to clear up energy from the past. Today, we will focus on relationships.

You have so many relationships in your life. Whether it's a romantic partner, friendships, business associates, family, and even acquaintances, your life is one big sum of relationships. As humans, we are relational beings. We thrive off of relationships.

With being relational beings, comes positive and negative consequences. On the positive side, relationships give us the opportunity to connect with others. Connection makes us feel alive and present. We feel energetic, happy and abundant when we have meaningful relationships. When we are happy with our relationships, we feel more confident and are unstoppable. We feel safe and grounded when we are surrounded by others who truly get us.

As amazing and beneficial as our relationships are, they are also the place where most of us hold our emotional ties. Since we are relational beings, most of us base our worth on relationships. We learn how to be ourselves through relationships. For the first few years of our life, we base ourselves on our parents and primary caregivers. As we go through life, we learn about ourselves through friendships, romantic partners, acquaintances and so forth.

Since relationships shape so much of who we are, we are also heavily affected by our relationships. When a relationship is not going well, it seems that our world falls apart. We feel insecure, doubtful and bad about ourselves. Especially if we have been hurt in a relationship, we take the hurt to our core, Since we base a lot of our worth on relationships, they have the potential to really affect our confidence.

The purpose of this workbook is to help you base your confidence less on your relationships with others, and more on your relationship with yourself.

However, I also want you to be mindful of the relationships you keep in your life. You are a relational being, so you will always be in relationships with others. Let's make sure they are the right relationships, the relationships that help you stay confident and true to yourself.

Your relationships have the power to make or break your confidence. This sounds dramatic, but it's true!

When you are surrounded by positive and uplifting relationships, you are able to fully be yourself and in your confident nature. Positive relationships have the power to uplift your spirit and help you become more of yourself.

Negative relationships on the other hand have the power to drain your energy and confidence. When you are surrounded by the wrong people, your confidence takes a hit. As the famous quote goes, you are the sum of the five people you spend the most time with. Let's make sure that these five relationships are quality ones that increase your confidence.

Today's focus is all about examining and clearing all of your relationships. You are highly impacted by the people you are around, so I want you to really understand the importance of decluttering your circle.

Who are you hanging around with? Are they adding or subtracting from your life? I want you to take an honest appraisal of everyone that is in your life today. I want you to think about each of your relationships and how they are affecting your confidence.

This is difficult work, no doubt. It can be difficult to be honest with yourself and be real about certain relationships. It's painful to realize that certain relationships are no longer good for you.

Having confidence comes with valuing positive relationships in your life. As difficult as it may be to disconnect from some people, it's crucial for your wellbeing.

Keep in mind, it's not about how many relationships you have. It's not about quantity, it's about quality. Your relationships need to be of high quality. If they don't have substance, they are not adding to your life. Your self love and confidence depend on your relationships.

Now in terms of romantic relationships, it can be very difficult to let go of a partner that may not be good for you. This is the predicament I was in a few years back, so I get it!

I want you to always remember that your partner should add to your life and not subtract from it. If your partner makes you feel insecure or doubtful, are you with the right person? If you have doubts, don't stuff them down. Pay attention to your intuition. Your partner should be your biggest supporter. They should give you the confidence to be yourself. If you are with someone who drains your energy and makes you feel bad about yourself, you are likely in the wrong relationship. You are worthy of such incredible love, remember that.

When we accept poor behavior from others in any relationship, we chip away at our self esteem and confidence. Part of having self love has to do with upholding your boundaries and making positive choices in relationships. That comes with releasing anyone who is not adding to your life.

When you decide to intentionally choose the relationships you are in, you instantly feel more confident in yourself. You realize that YOU have the power in your relationships. You choose who you are surrounding yourself with. You surround yourself with positive vibes. You make the choices.

Today's lesson is all about taking an inventory of your current relationships and releasing the ones that aren't adding to your life. Now, how do you release relationships?

Here's my best advice when it comes to clearing relationships. Clearing relationships does not mean that you are automatically cutting people out of your life. This is not meant to be vindictive or hurtful to anyone.

Clearing and releasing relationships is more about deciding to detach from the relationship, to give yourself some space. In some cases, clearing relationships means that you cut off contact, such as when breaking up with a toxic partner. In other cases, you learn to set boundaries, which will be discussed tomorrow. You may also choose to give yourself some distance, to get some space, to communicate your feelings and to develop better boundaries.

Do what feels right to you. The lesson of the day is to be mindful of your relationships, so you surround yourself with others who uplift your spirit and confidence.

Day 6 Reflection

Relationship inventory time, are there relationships in your life that are draining? Subtracting from your life?

Are there certain relationships that you need to completely cut off?

What is your action plan for dealing with
relationships that drain you?
*(Ex: getting distance, setting boundaries, communicating
concerns)*

How does it feel to start decluttering your
relationships?

What positive relationships are you thankful for in your life?

How has it felt to take an honest look at your relationships today?

Day 7:

Setting Boundaries

Welcome to Day 7! At this point, you have done a lot of transformational work in developing your confidence. Let's keep the journey going.

Yesterday, I helped you get real about your relationships and take an honest appraisal of each one. Decluttering your relationships is a process you should engage in every so often. It's always important to keep your circle tight and right. Always ask yourself, is my circle adding to my life or subtracting from it? From there, you will know what to do.

Today, I want to help you learn a crucial skill that will help in all aspects of your life, especially with your confidence. This skill is learning how to set boundaries.

What are boundaries? Boundaries are the rules and principles you live by. They govern what you will and won't allow in your life.

There are physical, emotional, mental, sexual and spiritual boundaries. Your boundaries are your rules and standards,. It's important to note that your boundaries are your own. Your boundaries will be different than mine, which is totally fine. These are your rules, and they are meant to be fully respected.

Boundaries can be a difficult topic to come across for many people. It's hard for a lot of us to set boundaries, for many reasons.

If you've had a difficult time with boundary setting, it can be because you often put the needs of others before your own, you are a people pleaser, you don't feel like you have the right to set boundaries, or you fear that boundaries will jeopardize your relationships. We fear that others will think we are stuck up and rude.

Even worse, setting boundaries means that we risk the possibility of rejection. Is there anything scarier than rejection to our egos? Probably not, which is why it can feel so difficult to set boundaries.

Setting boundaries can be uncomfortable, but it's crucial to your confidence and quality of life. Think of your boundaries as your barrier of protection. By setting boundaries, you'll get to witness who respects them and who simply doesn't.

As difficult as it can be to set boundaries, it's even more difficult to have your boundaries disrespected. Letting others step over your boundaries makes you feel powerless, insecure and lost. Think about the last time someone disregarded what you felt and did what they wanted, how did you feel? Did that make you feel good about yourself? I am strongly guessing that it didn't.

When we don't uphold our boundaries, we can fall victim to others who are abusive and disrespectful. We start to become a passive observer in our own lives, allowing others to walk over us. We lose touch of who we really are. This eats away at our confidence.

If you are struggling with your confidence, I am certain that you've been in a situation where your boundaries were disregarded. This could have been in an intimate relationship or a close friendship. It could have been in your family. It could have happened at work..

Having confidence has to do with setting your own boundaries and being firm with them. It's knowing that no matter what anyone else thinks, you are going to stay by your boundaries. You will constantly be tested by others. The trick is, can you stick with your boundaries? Can you be firm and assertive with your needs? This is the ultimate test of confidence.

The art of setting boundaries will require saying no at times. This is necessary. Don't allow rejection to scare you. From here on out, I want you to understand that rejection is a redirection. Yes, some people may reject you when you have boundaries, but you don't want those people in your life anyways. The people who are meant to be in your life will respect your boundaries, no questions asked.

The million dollar question is, how do you set your own boundaries?

The first step is to become crystal clear about what you will and won't allow in your life. As you will complete in the exercise today, you will be asked to think about different aspects of your life and what your boundaries are. Make sure you are clear when it comes to your boundaries because they will be tested throughout your life.

After you are clear about your boundaries, comes the difficult part, upholding it! Now that you know what you will and won't allow in your life, you will go about your life. As will always happen, your boundaries will be crossed at some point in life.

Now, the magic happens when someone crosses your boundaries. When you start to set boundaries, people may cross them unintentionally. This is normal and will happen, so expect it. This is the perfect opportunity to communicate what your boundaries are.

You communicate your boundaries calmly, in an assertive way. You set boundaries by communicating your needs and telling people what you will allow in your life. Remember that this is not an excuse to get angry at others or punish them. We can't expect others to read our minds and know what our boundaries are.

Now comes the true test. It's all about how the person in front of you reacts to your boundaries. Do they respect it or do they try to walk all over it it? Do they laugh at it and act like it's not a big deal? Or do they try to understand you and respect your boundaries? Here's the true test of how this person feels about you.

People who respect you will respect your boundaries. They will try their best to respect you. No questions asked. If you set a boundary and it is getting disregarded, that person is testing you and does not respect your boundaries. In any relationship, you have the right to be respected for your boundaries. If your boundaries are being disregarded, that is not the relationship for you.

It takes time and relearning to be able to set your boundaries. Practice makes perfect, which is why you have this guide! The more you set your boundaries and uphold them, the more confident you will become.

When you realize that others can't walk all over you, you grow confidence and self love for yourself. There is no better confidence boost than being able to stand up for yourself in a calm and assertive way.

Remember, you grow your self love by setting boundaries. You start to choose YOURSELF. You treat yourself with love and respect. You learn to respect yourself on a deep level.

For today's reflection, I really want you to become crystal clear on what your boundaries are, in all aspects of your life. Whether it's setting aside one hour each day where you are uninterrupted by your family, or setting the boundary that you will finally take breaks at work, or deciding not to be intimate with someone until you are in a relationship, get used to thinking about your boundaries.

Your boundaries don't have to be big and scary declarations; they can be as simple as taking an hour nap each day, having some more alone time at work, or limiting how much you talk to your nagging friend. They can be as simple or as grand as you like.

This is a chance for you to really understand what is important for you. The art of setting boundaries was truly revolutionary for me. It helped me understand what my needs and wants were.

It made me confident in all aspects of life, as I knew what was acceptable and what wasn't. It helped me be myself. It helped me recognize who truly respected me and who didn't. The art of setting boundaries really helped me develop inner confidence on a deep level.

Examples of Boundaries;

I will not work past my time at work.
I will give myself 30 minutes each day to watch my favorite show.
I will give myself space when I come home from work, and let my significant other know that this is what I need.
I will respect my sexual boundaries and not become intimate with someone until we are in a relationship.
I will not spend hours on the phone gossiping.
I will say "No" to events I don't want to go to.

Day 7 Reflection

List some boundaries that you need to set in the different aspects of your life.

Personal Life:

Family/Friendships:

Relationships:

Work:

Are there specific people you struggle setting boundaries with? List how you can better improve your boundaries with them below.

What specific actions can you take to improve your boundaries?

How will you handle boundary violations?

How does it feel to get clear about your boundaries?

Day 8:

monitor your words

Today's lesson is all about becoming aware of your spoken word. When it comes to being confident and more self loving towards yourself, you have to get used to monitoring the words that come out of your mouth!

It's so important to become more aware of your words and what you put out into the Universe. You may think that words mean nothing, but they hold tremendous power.

Whether it's the words you say out loud or your inner self talk (your thoughts), it's important to change the language you use.

When we struggle with self love and confidence, our self talk is usually very negative. It definitely was for me. You may have very negative thoughts about yourself. Your failures may constantly be in your thoughts. You may use derogatory words to describe yourself. You may complain a lot and talk about what's wrong in your life. You may engage in gossip.

Whatever it is, there is a definite connection between your language and your confidence level. The words you think and say impact every single one of your experiences.

As a therapist and a mindset coach, I use the Law of Attraction (LOA) in my teachings. You may have heard of the LOA as well. In any case, the LOA states that our thoughts are always attracting back similar thoughts.

To put it basically, your thoughts are always manifesting. When you have negative thoughts, you are attracting back negative thoughts and experiences. When you have positive thoughts, you are attracting back positive thoughts and experiences.

You may have thought that negative thoughts toward yourself have no effect on your confidence. That's actually not the truth! When you direct your negative thoughts to yourself, you attract similar situations that will make you feel negative. See how this works? It's all a self fulfilling prophecy. What you put out into the Universe, you will get back. So, the words that you put out will always come back to you.

You live and die by your tongue. Dramatic much, but it's true. You can either speak words that add to your life or subtract from it. Having confidence comes with monitoring the language you use, the thoughts you have about yourself, and the spoken word.

For example, if you constantly tell yourself you are ugly and fat, how do you think you will feel about yourself? Will you be in a good mood? Will you feel good about yourself? My guess is that you won't. Those words will bring your spirit down and bring you to a low energetic space. From that space, you attract similar thoughts, feelings and situations.

This is why the individual who says "I am so

unlucky, I am always in bad relationships" will have a very difficult time attracting positive relationships! What you speak will always manifest. When you focus on the negative and how unlucky you are, that's exactly what you will attract back into your life.

Make it a habit starting today to always talk about what you want to manifest in your life. If you want to manifest a relationship, don't talk about how bad men are and how you are so unlucky in love. Break the negative pattern. Talk about how you are excited for love and ready to meet your soulmate. Talk about the positive couples around you. Start to tune into happy relationships. Whatever it is, talk about what you WANT to manifest.

Today's focus will be on the spoken word, as it is something you can change today. You can begin to monitor the words you say out of your mouth, right this second. This will make such a difference in the way you feel about yourself. In fact, if it's one thing you learn from this book that will change your life immediately, it's this skill.

Even on your bad days, I want you to monitor your words and the conversations you choose to have. When things are not going well, practice the art of not talking about it. This means, you don't have to spend all day talking about your problems and venting about it to your friends. As difficult as this may be, it's crucial. Detach from the problem by taking your attention away from it. Focus on the solution. Focus on how you can fix the situation.

The next time you want to say anything out loud, ask yourself, *is what I am saying something I want to manifest into my life?* If it is, then great, say it away! If it's not, it's time to stop yourself and not say anything. Yes, do not say it. Swallow your words.

By becoming more aware of the words you speak, you feel better. You start to gain confidence and self love. Remember that the self loving version of yourself does not speak negatively about herself.

So, if you want to develop irresistible confidence and self love, you have to constantly monitor your words. Constantly watch what is coming out of your mouth. You are so much more than the words you have been attaching to yourself. From today on, speak in loving and positive terms about yourself.

Day 8 Reflection

Take this moment to monitor your language, how would you describe the words you speak about yourself? Are they mostly negative or positive?

Are there any negative thoughts or words you repeat about yourself often?

How can you commit to monitoring your words and being more loving to yourself?

What can you do the next time you are tempted to say something negative about yourself?

List 10 positive thoughts about yourself right now.

Day 9:

Love Rampage

Day 9 is all about you and the qualities you love about yourself. I am so excited about today! Since we have uncovered and released the "heavier" stuff, it's time to get into the fun stuff!

Yesterday, you learned about the importance of monitoring your language. This is a skill that you can start to implement right away, and it is crucial on your your way to having unshakeable confidence.

During this self help journey, practice and consistency will be key. A lot of the material may seem difficult to apply at first, so don't be too hard on yourself. Keep practicing each of the skills we talk about, and they will become like second nature.

It's time to go on a love rampage today, on yourself! Today is all about focusing on all the positive qualities you have.

No matter how you your confidence is at this point, we both know that you have so many amazing qualities. Qualities that others love about you. Qualities that make you unique. In fact, I know for a fact that you have so many positive qualities. I'm thrilled to help you uncover your positive qualities today.

No matter what has happened in the past, you are lovable. I know it can be difficult to feel that you are lovable, but you are. Purely for being alive, are you lovable and worthy of all life has to offer.

God, the Universe, your Higher Power absolutely loves you. You are an infinite being of love. Your true essence is love, so it's time we bring that out.

When we have our insecure goggles on, we lose track of all we have to offer. We forget about our positive qualities. We forget that we are infinite beings of love. Put frankly, we forget about who we really are at our core. At your core, you are love, and you have forgotten that.

Insecurities arise when you lose track of all the love you have in you. You have spent so much time focusing on what you don't like about yourself. This makes you lose track of all that you love about yourself.

Having self love and confidence comes with loving yourself, flaws and all. As cliche as it sounds, loving yourself will change your life dramatically. There is only one of you. You are special and unique. You are made of love.

By this point you have forgiven yourself for past mistakes and experiences. You have worked on releasing the past. You have analyzed your relationships. You have worked on forgiving others and clearing the past. You have cleared the physical and energetic space for self love to come in.

It's now time to get to love yourself on a deeper level. Over the next few days, I'll help you get in touch with who you really are, at your core. I'll help you be kind to yourself and express love towards yourself. As cliche as this may sound, I promise it works when it comes to developing your confidence.

Tuning in to what you love about yourself is a powerful way to invite more love into your life. Love is the purest vibration. Once you turn that love on yourself, you will attract love into your life in many ways.

Remember, by the Law of Attraction, you are always attracting that which you think. The more loving thoughts you think about yourself, the more loving thoughts, feelings and experiences you will attract.

For the reflection questions today, you are going to go on a love rampage, towards the best person in the world, yourself.

Day 9 Reflection

Go on a love rampage. List as many qualities as possible that you love about yourself. If you are having a difficult time, ask yourself, what would a friend say they love about you?

What makes you unique? What are your unique
talents, gifts, interests or hobbies?

What do you appreciate about yourself the most?

What would your loved ones say they love the most about you?

What do you think are your best qualities?

What can you do to remind yourself of your positive qualities throughout the day?

Day 10:

Own your Strengths

Here we are at Day 10! Welcome to another day that is going to focus on all of your amazing qualities. I hope you are used to talking positively about yourself, because there is more of that today.

In order to be the most confident you to date, you need to elevate the way you see yourself. This comes from monitoring your language, speaking positively about yourself, and appreciating all of the amazing qualities you have.

This may feel uncomfortable for you, especially if you're used to speaking about yourself in a negative way. Don't worry if this is the case, because it takes time to develop these new skills. Remember that confidence is a habit that you are cultivating into your life. Even if you feel uncomfortable doing these exercises, keep doing them. With practice, you will feel more and more comfortable.

Now that you were able to take note of your positive qualities during yesterday's lesson, I hope that you are beginning to feel better about yourself. Increasing your self love comes from being appreciative of yourself and what makes you special. When you learn to love the qualities you possess, you begin to rebuild your self love and confidence.

Today, we are going to continue to focus on the positive qualities you have to offer. Except, we are going to talk about your strengths and what specific skills you have. Today's motive is to rebuild the way you view yourself and your skills, in the different aspects of your life.

You've heard the word strength ever since you were a child, but what actually are strengths? Your strengths are the qualities and skills you have that you excel at. They usually come easily for you and are many times second nature. You use these abilities to function in your daily life, work, relate with others, and achieve goals. These are the skills you have that set you apart from others.

We each have our own unique strengths. My strengths are different than yours. This is what makes our world so lovely and unique, we all have different strengths.

Your strengths will usually come very naturally to you. It will be a skill or talent you have that is second nature for you. For example, maybe you are naturally good at math, or maybe you are an excellent dancer. You may be gifted with communication and relating to people. You may be gifted with writing and expressing yourself. Think of what you are naturally good at, which will give you a hint about your strengths.

In order to build your confidence, you need to tune in to your strengths. By becoming aware of your strengths, you become more confident about your abilities. You know what you are good at. You start to identify with your skills. This helps you become more assured and confident, because you know yourself. Knowing your strengths also helps you in decision making, a topic which we will discuss on a later day.

By knowing what you're good at, you can develop confidence in yourself. For example, I know I am not a good athlete, like at all! By knowing this about myself, I stay away from playing sports, and instead focus on watching them. I love watching sports, but I am aware that I am not the athlete of my city. However, my self esteem is not affected, because I know what my strengths are. Playing basketball is not my forte, but so many other things are. By knowing what my strengths are, I know what I am good at and what I'm not so good at. This helps me have a strong sense of self because I know my abilities.

When I am around other athletes, I praise them and am in awe of them. I can do this while feeling extremely self loving and assured of myself. This is exactly what confidence is; knowing who you are and loving yourself for all that you are.

I want the same for you. You are going to reach a point where you are so confident, that you have no time to find faults in yourself. Even when you are faced with a weakness, which we all have, you won't feel insecure anymore.

When I was insecure, I would feel so embarrassed or disappointed if I wasn't good at something. It would ruin my day and make me doubt myself. Why did I feel that way? It was because I didn't know who I was and what my skills were. I didn't realize what I was good at. This made me focus on all that I couldn't do.

The goal of today is to get you to recognize your strengths, so that you never feel bad about your abilities again. Now of course, you will have your weaknesses (discussed tomorrow), but by owning what they are, you won't feel insecure again about them.

The exercises designed for today are going to be all about identifying and owning your strengths. I want you to begin to identify your strengths and own who you are. You may be used to being in the shadows right now, but that's all going to change here! You have strengths and I want you to put them center stage. I want you to be proud of them and share it with others when appropriate.

I want to make note that the focus of today is on your internal strengths, meaning they come from you. Look at the different types of strengths below and start to think about the ones you have.

Personality Traits - Traits that you have that you view are beneficial.

Ex: Being caring, confident, kind, empathic, kind hearted

Experience — Experience or expertise you have in a particular area of life, field, job & on.

Ex: Experience working as a hairdresser for 20 years.

Talents — A special ability you have, often an athlete, creative or artistic aptitude.

Ex: Being an amazing athlete, being a natural born cook, knowing how to sow

Education/Training — Education/training you have in a specific field or industry.

Ex: Degrees, certifications, special training

Interests - Areas or topics that you are passionate about.

Ex: such as hobbies, particular hobbies, particular topics of conversation & on.

Resources - This is the only strength that is external, meaning that it has to do with your environment. Resources can be depleted when fully used.

Ex: Your resources are your external strengths, such as your relationships, family environment, financial status, job & on.

Day 10 Reflection

What are the personality traits you have that you view as a strength?

What experience or expertise do you have?

What are your talents?

Any specialized education/training?

What are your interests and hobbies?

What external resources do you have in your environment?

How does it feel to know that you have so much internal value?

Day 11: Accepting your weaknesses

Hello Day 11! Yesterday's lesson was all about your strengths. I hope you learned some valuable information about yourself.

Knowing your strengths will help you in all aspects of your life. When you are feeling down or having a difficult day, remind yourself of your strengths and all that you have to offer. That will help you elevate your vibration and get you to a better feeling place.

With strengths, comes weaknesses. Weaknesses are not exactly a bad thing, which is why I believe it's so important to dedicate a chapter to this concept.

You see love, just like we all have strengths, we all have weaknesses. It's human nature. Yes, even Beyonce and JLO have weaknesses, as much as they seem like they don't! It's human nature, and something that you will learn to embrace in this lesson.

The most confident people in the world have weaknesses. Do you know what the difference is between insecure and confident people? Confident people embrace their weaknesses. They work around their weaknesses in such a way, that it becomes an asset for them.

What can I possibly mean by this? Imagine you are a top level business woman. You run your own company, travel all over the world, and bring in millions yearly. Your life looks almost perfect and you have people all over the world who admire your brand. At the same time, you are clumsy, suck at time management, and need help with your bookkeeping. You can't keep track of all you need to do and need assistance when it comes to organization.

Being the confident businesswoman that you are, you don't take your organizational difficulties as a bad omen of what's going to happen to your business. Not at all! In fact, you embrace them and instead decide that it's best to hire help. You hire an assistant to keep you organized. You hire a bookkeeper. Perfect, you are all set. Your business improves because you took action. You looked for the solution, which helped you become even more successful.

As the confident you that you are, you don't freak out that your organizational skills are not on point. You know that it's a weak spot. Instead of getting down on yourself about it, you take action and take the necessary steps to find the solution.

This is the major difference between being insecure and being confident. When you are insecure, you take your weaknesses and run with them. You feel like a failure. You want to give up. You think you suck at everything. You lose your drive. When you are confident, you take your weaknesses with a grain of salt. Instead of feeling bad about yourself, you look for the solution.

So, in order to have a full understanding of all that you are, you need to take into account your weaknesses. Weakness is not a negative or derogatory word. In fact, a weakness just represents a skill or task that may not come second nature to you. It's an area of life you need a little more help in. That's pretty much all that a weakness is in this guide.

Acknowledging and accepting your weaknesses makes you unstoppable. I want you to understand that your weaknesses are not your downfall. They are simply the areas that you may need some help and improvement in. By knowing your weaknesses, you know how to find the solution.

Personally, there are so many tasks that are not my forte when it comes to my business. Certain technical tasks don't come second nature to me. It's so much easier for me to outsource these tasks, then to spend hours trying to do them myself. By knowing this about myself, I can save myself time, stress and productivity.

So, the moral of this chapter is that knowing your weaknesses gives you a better understanding of yourself and how you function. From that place, you can proceed to find the solution. Identifying your weaknesses contributes to your growth and confidence. The more aware you are of your weaknesses, the better decisions you can make. You are less likely to put yourself in situations that are frustrating, and you save more time, energy and productivity.

Today, I want you to acknowledge and accept your weaknesses. This will make you feel confident in your abilities, in what you can and can't do. This way, you will never be surprised or stunned when any problem arises. You will know how to handle challenges and difficulties, because you are already aware of them.

Confidence does not equate to perfection. This is what I hope you understand in this book. Confidence comes with accepting who you are and loving ALL that you are, strengths and weaknesses alike. The truly confident woman is not perfect and she doesn't want to be. She just wants to be herself.

Day 11 Reflection

Think of the "weaknesses" that you have that make you feel insecure.
Ex; Not being a good writer, not being a good athlete

How can you look for a solution to your weaknesses?

How does understanding your weaknesses better
help you prepare for the future?

Are you able to accept your weaknesses? Can you
come to terms with the fact that you can't be
perfect?

Below, I want you to accept all of the weaknesses from above. Write it as an affirmation and repeat it to yourself as often as you can today.

Ex: Today, I accept that I am not the best writer, and that's perfectly fine!

Today, I accept that..

What are the strengths you have opposite to your weaknesses?

Do you feel confident as you identify your strengths and weaknesses?

Day 12: Gratitude

Gratitude for ourselves, our surroundings, and our life is extremely important on our journey towards self love. Gratitude is so important in all aspects of your life, but especially when it comes to your confidence.

I'm sure you've heard the word gratitude thrown around 100000 times in the personal development world. It's such a popular topic for good reason. You'll hear people from all walks of life talk about the importance of gratitude. Today, you'll learn about why gratitude is so important in terms of your confidence.

Why gratitude? To put it simply, being grateful opens the door to have more to be grateful for. When you genuinely appreciate what you have in your life, the Universe will always reward you with more. To get more from life, you first have to be thankful for the present moment.

If you are not feeling grateful for your present moment, how can you expect your life to improve? Remember that the Universe is always matching your vibration. The better you feel, the better thoughts, feelings and situations you will attract.

I understand how difficult it could be to be grateful when you are feeling stuck and unhappy in your life. The last thing you feel is appreciative of your insecure status. You are dreaming of a time where you will have a lot to be grateful for. However, it doesn't work that way! In order to live that life you want, you need to find a way to be grateful right now.

You are a beautiful being. You are alive. You are able to read the words on this page. You are interested in your personal development. You value your confidence. You have money that can buy you things. You have food on the table. You are able to breathe and be alive. You are much more lucky than you think.

The most confident version of yourself feels grateful for the big and little things. Gratitude is not just about being grateful for the big accomplishments in your life. Yes, it's easy to be grateful when you are making millions or are with your soulmate, but what about in your simple day to day moments? Gratitude is about the small moments. It's about being thankful for the simplicities we often overlook.

To be confident, you need to get into the habit of being genuinely grateful for your life. This may be difficult right now, but start with the small things. What are you genuinely thankful for right now? What makes you happy today? What brings a smile to your face? Make sure that it's genuine.

What helped me become more confident was doing a gratitude exercise each morning. I still do this ritual today! A gratitude exercise is an amazing way to tune into all that you appreciate in your life. I think this exercise is so powerful, that it's worth going over today.

Gratitude Exercise

This exercise is so simple, but so transformational when done! I recommend picking a time each day when you will do your gratitude exercise. Simply write or recite to yourself 5 things you are grateful for each day. That's it.

Most people choose to do this in the morning or right before bed, but it really doesn't matter when you do it. The important factor is to do your gratitude exercise daily, even if you do it at different times of the day. As you do this daily, you will start feel better about yourself. You will be tuning into all that you are appreciative for in your life. This will activate positive energy in you, which will in turn attract similar frequencies into your life. This simple exercise can create an avalanche of positivity.

What's even more important in all of this, is to make sure that your gratitude list is genuine. Don't just write things down that you think you should be grateful for. Write down what you are truly grateful for.

Gratitude leads to self love, confidence and happiness. When you start to appreciate what's around you, you get into the habit of speaking about the positivity around you. This increases your self love and self esteem. When you realize all you have to be grateful for, all that you've accomplished or what others have done for you, you become more confident.

You retrain your brain to focus on the good of the day, which helps you naturally become a more confident person. More positive thoughts leads to positive feelings which leads to self love and confidence. Try this task out every day and watch how your life changes.

Gratitude List

List 25 things you are grateful for below. List more if you can.

Can you commit to starting a gratitude practice every day?

Make a commitment to yourself about when you will start your gratitude practice. Will you journal it or recite it? Will you do it during morning or night?

How did it feel to write down your gratitude list? What emotions are you feeling right now?

Day 13: Self Care

Day 13 here we are! You have almost been on this journey for two weeks, which is amazing! You have done so much work in the past few weeks.

I hope you are seeing a shift in your confidence. At this point, you have learned about so many new concepts and skills. Try to regularly check in with yourself to gage how you feel.

These next few days will be lighter emotionally (I am sure you are excited about this), but they will be just as important. For the next few days, we are going to dive into the importance of making time for yourself, trying new activities, taking part in self care and finding your passions. These next few days will be fun and interesting, as having confidence is all about tending to your needs and finding what makes you unique.

The most confident version of yourself prioritizes herself, always. She realizes that she is the most important person in her life. She takes care of herself. She checks in with herself and makes sure that she isn't burned out.

When you take care of yourself, you actually become a more selfless person. You have nothing to offer anyone if you are not taking care of yourself. Remember this! You can't pour from an empty cup.

Prioritizing yourself is the ultimate way to develop selflessness and give back to others. When you feel full and happy, you are more likely to give that love to others. This kills two birds with one stone.

Now, your self care is always a priority, no matter how busy you are. Actually, if you are a very busy woman, self care is even more important! The busier you get, the more you need to check on yourself and your needs.

Adding self care routines into your daily life makes you feel happier, more fulfilled and ready to give to others. Without doing so, you will be frazzled like that mother above.

So let's get into it, what is self care?

Self care is any activity that you do to take care of your emotional, mental and physical health. To put simply, it's to care for yourself. It's about identifying what your needs are emotionally, mentally and physically. Once you identify your needs, it's important to make time for yourself to meet them.

Self care has so many benefits. In regards to your confidence, when you regularly make time for yourself for self care purposes, you send a strong message to your subconscious mind that you are worthy and important. You treat yourself like you matter. This will help you silence your inner critics and negative self talk.

To name a few other advantages of self care, it enhances your self esteem, increases your productivity, elevates your mood, increases your self awareness, and enhances your life. I think it's obvious how important self care is to your life!

There are different levels of self care that I am going to have you focus on today. Let's go over them.

Physical self care involves your physical needs. This can be taking care of your body, exercising, eating right, getting a massage, taking a nice bath and on. This type of self care is an activity that you do to take care of a need. For example, when I am feeling tired, I love to take a shower. This is the ultimate act of self care for me. I feel very relaxed and at peace after I take a hot shower. This is a great example of physical self care.

Emotional self care has to do with identifying, accepting and expressing your emotional needs. This involves giving yourself the time to process and sort through your emotional needs. You can take care of yourself emotionally in many ways. The goal is to somehow be able to express your emotions. You can have a conversation about your needs. You can set boundaries. You can journal your feelings. You can also draw, color, listen to music, play an instrument, write, journal and on in order to express your feelings. The act can be physical, but you are emotionally tuning in to your feelings and needs.

Spiritual self care is an exploration of your beliefs and values. Spirituality has a different meaning for everyone. I think of spirituality as being in connection with your soul. Do you feel connected with your soul? Do you know your purpose? No matter what you believe in, I am sure that you have a spiritual connection of some sort. Spirituality doesn't tie to religion, even though it can for you. It's connecting to a higher purpose. You can take care of your spiritual needs by practicing religion, observing nature, meditating, journaling, tapping into your spirituality and so on.

Social self care involves tending to your relational needs. We often get so bogged down by responsibilities. It seems like most of us are always working! While it is amazing to have dedication and persistence in work, it's just as important to nurture relationships with others. We often put our relationships on the back burner, especially when we get into relationships or have children. Humans are extremely relational beings. We thrive off of relationships. Social self care means nursing your relationships and taking time to be with your loved ones. Research shows that our relationships are very important to our overall wellbeing. Being around amazing friends and family also helps us feel more confident and loved. When you tend to your relationships, you tend to your social needs.

As you can see, there are SO many options for self care acts you can add to your daily life. To give you a few tips for adding self care into your routine, I want to remind you that this is not to overwhelm you. Your self care activities should be fun. They should be activities you look forward to! I know for me, I absolutely look forward to my weekly massages in pure excitement. That's how your self care activity should feel for you.

Adding self care activities into your day can be simple. Stick to the basics for now. You will find your own rhythm and routine. Your self care can be as simple as taking a hot shower or taking 30 minutes a night to watch your favorite show.

Self care works best when you actively plan it into your schedule. It's an active choice and you have to start treating it as such. I recommend planning the days in your week that you are going to engage in your self care activities. Add activities to your calendar, tell your plans to others, and look for opportunities to add it to your daily life.

Self care increases your confidence in many ways. When you are taking care of yourself in these different ways, you are showing love to yourself. We take care of people we love, and you taking care of yourself is just as loving.

When you begin to meet your own needs, you realize that you have the power to take care of yourself. You start to become more confident in your ability to take care of yourself and others. Self care also communicates to you and others that you are valuable and important. By placing a value on yourself, you teach people how to treat you.

Day 13 Reflection

List the self care activities you enjoy for these different categories.

Physical Self Care:

Emotional Self Care:

Spiritual Self Care:

Social Self Care:

What self care activity can you commit to completing today? This week? Make a schedule for yourself below.

How can you commit to adding self care to your routine?

How can self care help you feel more confident and empowered?

Day 14: Step Outside your Comfort Zone

I hope you were able to engage in much needed self care yesterday. It's so important to take care of your needs. I hope yesterday's lesson has inspired you to make your self care a priority.

Along the lines of self care, Day 14 is all about stepping out of your comfort zone. Today's lesson will teach you the importance of trying new things and stepping away from your comfort zone. I'll explain to you why it's so important to constantly challenge yourself. Confidence comes from trying new things and doing things before you are ready.

Your comfort zone is your default comfortable space. This can be a thought, feeling, place, behavior or thing. Your comfort zone is your safety net, where you feel the least challenged.

For example, you may be comfortable with feeling insecure and doubtful. You may be used to having low self esteem. You may feel like it's better to stay at your safe job than to try out the entrepreneur route. You may stay with a partner for the sake of comfort. Whatever the case is, your comfort zone keeps you stagnant and where your ego feels the most safe.

Your ego is the part of your mind that wants you to be comfortable and protected. Your ego wants you to feel "safe". Your ego tries to protect you by making you fear the unknown and what's out there for you. This is why it's so easy to stay in bad relationships or stay at a job you hate for 20 years.

It's the same reason that feeling insecure often is a comfort zone for many people, because they know what to expect. Ironically, staying in your comfort zone is not the safe decision; it's the decision that leads to feeling stuck and stagnant.

You feel a false sense of security in your comfort zone. You may think that it's a great place to be and a comfortable feeling, but it stagnates your growth. Just because your ego wants to protect you, does not mean that the protection is for your highest good.

Your comfort zone can trap you for many reasons.

1. It's comfortable and you know what to expect.
2. It's out of habit.
3. It's easier to stay in your comfort zone.
4. It feels uncomfortable to change, so you rather stay where you are comfortable.
5. It makes you believe that you are powerless to make change.
6. It keeps you small.
7. It keeps you stuck in the past.
8. It makes you feel insecure, doubtful and frustrated with yourself.
9. It robs you of life.
10. It leads you to unhappiness later on in life, as you always wonder "What if I followed my dreams?"

If you want to build your confidence and self love, it's time to step outside of your comfort zone. Becoming more confident comes with taking risks. It comes with stepping outside of your familiar bubble and trying something new.

It's scary at first to try something new and put yourself out there. I remember how scared I was when I first started my business! Then, when I made the decision to become more public, I remember feeling just as scared. At different levels, come different fears. If I had listened to my fears and stayed in my comfort zone, this book wouldn't exist. Positive Soul wouldn't exist and I wouldn't be able to help people all over the world. So, there's a lot of risk in staying in your comfort zone and playing it safe.

Stepping outside of your comfort zone can be any action that you have been putting off. This can be as simple as taking piano lessons, starting a blog, writing a book, engaging in public speaking, taking dancing lessons and so on.

The activity has to be new and a little bit scary. There has to be some "newness" involved. The way to develop your confidence comes from learning new skills. When you master a skill or take that class you always wanted to take, you become confident in yourself and your abilities.

There are two steps to getting out of your comfort zone.

1) The first step is that you decide that you are going to act. You decide to do something out of your comfort zone. This is an important step, because often deciding is the hardest step.

2) The second step is to actually get out there and do it. This can be enrolling in that class, signing up for that dance lesson and so forth. For me, when I decided to come out as Jacqueline for Positive Soul, I decided and committed to the day that I was going to do it. This scared me but made me feel so proud at the same time.

For today, I want you to follow step 1, which is to decide what you are going to do. Take time to think about an act which scares you and excites you at the same time. Then when you have the time, get out there and do it as step 2 states, as soon as you can.

As this book comes to an end, make sure that you are constantly challenging yourself to get out of your comfort zone. The enemy to success is stagnation. Push yourself to constantly be and do more. The ultimate way to develop confidence comes from mastering new skills and putting yourself out there to do more.

Day 14 Reflection

What makes up your comfort zone right now? What thoughts, feelings, behaviors or actions limit your growth?

What would you like to do to step outside of your comfort zone? Think of an activity or skill you've been wanting to learn.

Decide a plan of action to help you complete that task.

When can you commit to doing this by? Put a specific plan in place for the day, the program, and the time you will be doing it.

What emotions come up for you as you decide to step outside of your comfort zone?

Write down some goals that you can accomplish in the near future (outside of your comfort zone).

Day 15:

Finding your passions

Welcome to Day 15 gorgeous! Today is all about exploring and finding what your passions are. Finding your passion is extremely important when it comes to developing your confidence.

Passion is the energy that fills us with meaning, happiness and excitement. It's not by mistake that you hear so often, "Find something you are passionate about and do that". Passion is the energy that keeps us going. It's ultimately the driving force behind confidence, happiness and success.

A passion can be any activity or desire that you like to do, purely for the reason that it brings you joy. Your passions are the opposite of responsibilities. Your passions are fun for you and they bring you happiness. They excite you!

One of my passions is my business, Positive Soul. Yes, I know that I have a responsibility attached to it now, but it's still my passion! I absolutely love working with others and working on my brand. It brings me so much joy to be on here. Positive Soul was developed from my passion for helping others, which is why I believe it's so successful. If I didn't have such passion for my work, it would have been so easy for me to give up and move on. My passion is what keeps me going.

I also have many other passions beside my work, such as watching sports, personal development, Law of Attraction and so forth. You can have many different passions, some of which are completely unrelated to each other. As long as it lights you up and brings you joy, you're on the right path.

You may be aware of your passions right now, or you may be disconnected from them. If you feel confused or stuck about what your passion is, do not worry. With self exploration, you'll be able to identify what your passions are.

To find out what your passions are, I suggest to start thinking about what you enjoy doing or learning, simply for fun. Think of an activity that brings you pure excitement and joy. You don't need to be forced to do the activity, and you can spend hours upon hours taking part in it.

To give you some more help, think about what you liked to do as a child for fun. This is a really good tip for finding where your passions lie. You will be asked a bunch of questions today to explore your passions, and I am positive you will figure some of them out.

Pursuing your passions makes you feel confident and full of self love. When you are doing something you love, you feel better about yourself. You are more full of life. You feel fulfilled, which helps you connect to your true nature of love and vitality. The more fulfilled you feel, the more confident you will be.

Your life is worth living, not just for getting by. The daily stresses will drive you sick if you don't follow your passions. Getting too caught up in work, responsibilities of the house, or others will rob you of your life. The more you enjoy your life, the more confident you will feel.

By pursuing your passions, you once again choose yourself. You communicate to yourself that you have are valuable and worthy of enjoying your life. You also teach others how important it is to pursue your passions and choose yourself.

Once you answer the questions below, I want you to think about a passion that you can begin pursuing right now. The key is to commit to following through on your passions. Create a plan of action like you did for yesterday's exercise. The more you commit to your self care, the better you will feel about yourself.

Day 15 Reflection

What's an activity that brings you joy and fulfillment?

What books do you love to read?

What subjects do you love talking about?

What do you find yourself "Google"-ing the most?

What are you most interested in viewing on social media?

What activity makes you feel the happiest?

What did you enjoy doing as a kid for fun?

Reflect upon your answers above and list a few of your passions.

Which passion can you commit to fulfilling today or by the end of this week? Decide a plan of action.

How can you incorporate your passions into your daily life? Decide a plan of action.

Day 16:

Decision making

Day 16! Yesterday's lesson was all about finding your passion and making time for it in your daily life. Always make time for your passions and keep finding more!

Day 16 continues your confidence journey. Today's lesson is all about becoming the ultimate decision maker of your life.

When it comes to being confident, being decisive is an important trait to have. The most confident people make many decisions. They decide even if the decision is scary. They put themselves out there and develop confidence because of their decisiveness.

Making decisions is so important for your confidence. Feeling indecisive, not knowing which path to take and feeling doubtful about yourself keep you stagnant. If you struggle with decision making, it's definitely a confidence issue. When you don't feel confident about yourself, you have a difficult time making decisions. You feel that your decisions are always wrong. You worry that you're never making the right decision.

Ironically, the more decisions you make, the more confident you become. So, you need to start making more decisions, even if you are scared to do so. That's how you'll develop confidence, not the other way around. You can't get to genuine confidence by being indecisive and deciding that "some day" you'll start making decisions. You have to start making more decisions right now, and then your confidence will follow, I promise you.

Not making decisions is a slippery slope. You start to get used to not making choices. You become more indecisive. You don't ever feel "good enough" to make a choice. This leads to stagnation and staying in your comfort zone. This starts to spill over into other aspects of your life, such as your relationships, work life and so on.

Being a people pleaser and always being at the mercy of others can invite toxicity into your life. By not making choices and decisions, you invite toxic people into your space. There are some individuals who thrive off of the insecurity of others. Abusers and emotionally manipulative partners want to be with someone who doesn't have the ability to make choices. I never want you to go through a toxic relationship. By always being a people pleaser and not making choices, you more likely fall into the hands of toxic friends, lovers and acquaintances. As dramatic as this sounds, it can happen!

Whatever the situation is, by not making choices you are doing yourself a huge disservice. Being passive in your own life leads to passivity in friendships and relationships. The more you stuff down your desires, the more unhappy you will be.

Saying "No" is another aspect of making decisions. By making decisions, you also have the right to say no when you want to. We often think that we always need to please others and say yes to others. This is not true. Practice saying no to others, often and consistently. Don't go to events that make you feel bad. Don't hang around with that friend who makes you feel bad about yourself. Choose to say no when you want to!

For today, I want you to practice making decisions and sticking up for yourself. I want you to think about times in your life where you let others make decisions for you. *How did that feel? Did you feel insecure and small in that moment?* I never want you to feel like that again.

It sounds simple, but you will be amazed at how rapidly your self love and confidence will increase once you start to exert choice and decision. A truly confident person has no problem making decisions. They make decisions often and consistently. The decision may not be the right one, but at least they made a decision. The more you practice exercising choice, the more confident you grow in yourself. Assertiveness leads to more confidence, happiness and self love.

Day 16 Reflection

Have you struggled with making decisions in your life? List some of the struggles you have had.

How has it felt for you to take on a passive role? How has this affected your confidence?

Are you ready to make more decisions in your life?

What have you been saying "Yes" to that you've wanted to say "NO!" to?

How do you think you will feel once you start to make more decisions?

Day 17: Be you & Own Who you are

Welcome to Day 17! I can't believe that we are almost done with this 21 day journey.

You have done SO much work up to this point. I hope you feel proud for getting this far. I am so proud of you for doing the inner work needed to transform your self love and confidence.

Day 17 is all about owning who you are. Becoming a confident and loving goddess comes with being you and owning all aspects of yourself. It doesn't matter what anyone else thinks; when you accept yourself, you become the most confident person on the planet.

What does it mean to own who you are? Owning who you are means owning your strengths, your "flaws", your personality, your job, your looks, your interests, your quirks and on. You love yourself for all of who you are.

The most confident people in the world own who they are. Some of the most confident people can be considered very "odd" to others. They have a specific style of clothing, dress, makeup, style and on. They can be viewed as being out there and different by others, but it doesn't matter, because people are drawn to them!

For example, let's think about an artist such as Lady Gaga. She is known for her extravagant looks and makeup, a look that may be considered "odd" to others. However, she confidently owns her look and is confident in who she is. She is so confident that we can't help but love her and her eccentricities. It doesn't matter what she is wearing or if she walks out with a meat dress, LOL! Her confidence makes her lovable to many.

We can see this all over the entertainment industry. As humans, we are drawn to confident people who own who they are. These people are a breath of fresh air, because they show us that we can be loved for being ourselves.

By owning who you are, you grow your confidence and self love. You also become highly attractive and magnetic. This guide is all about your confidence, but I also quickly want to discuss how having confidence makes you irresistible to others. It has been proven psychologically that the most attractive quality someone can possess is confidence. Confidence is rated as even more attractive than physical looks. Crazy right? It's not a coincidence. When someone is confident, they communicate with others that they are valuable. They command respect and attention. Therefore, not only do you become more fulfilled with confidence, you also become very attractive to all those around you, a definite plus.

A confident person gets more opportunities in the workplace, in relationships, friendships and on. A confident person has an aura that others are drawn to, like a moth to a flame. As you develop your confidence, you will firsthand experience how your life will change. All of those things you wanted will make its way to you.

There's something exciting and fulfilling about standing up and claiming your place in this world. Are you ready to embrace yourself and own who you are? Who are you meant to be? Are you ready to stop giving a damn what others think and own it?

I want you to have clarity about who you are from this point forward. I want you to own your personality, your personal style, your interests, your passions and so forth. I want you to own your life mission. Own what you do for work. Own what your passions are. Be comfortable in your own skin.

This is your life. You don't find fulfillment and success by living in the shadows and doing what everyone else wants you to do. You become a confident person by making your own choices and doing what you want.

Once you start owning and accepting who you are, your confidence and self love will skyrocket. It will feel extraordinary to be you. You will feel sure of yourself no matter where you are or who you are with.

Don't fear being judged by others. People will judge you regardless of what you do. There will always be unhappy bystanders who will judge you, because they are unhappy with their lives. If you are afraid of judgment (which I was for years), remind yourself that judgment will always be there. You are going to be talked about regardless, so might as well do what you want!

How do you own who you are? You own who you are by accepting yourself. You start to be fully and authentically you. You let others get to know the real you You do your own thing and live your own truth.

You are an infinite being. There is only one of you. You are amazing and others want to get to know the real you. You are doing a disservice to yourself and those in your life when you hide who you really are. Be proud and let today be the day you finally show yourself to the world.

Day 17 Reflection

Who are you to your core? What makes you, you?

How have you been hiding yourself from others?
Why have you decided to hide?

How has the fear of being judged stopped you from fully living your life?

How would it feel to own who you are and finally show people the real you?

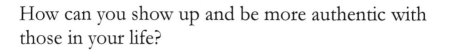

How can you show up and be more authentic with those in your life?

Below, write a love letter to yourself, owning who you are and being proud of how far you have come.

Day 18: Act as if

4 days to go! Today's lesson is all about playing the part of a confident and self loving person.

As I've talked about the Law of Attraction in previous chapters, you've heard me talk about how your thoughts attract similar thoughts into your life. Now, what better way to speed up your confidence by thinking, feeling and acting like the most confident version of yourself?

Acting like you are THAT girl will fast track your confidence.

You can feel the feeling of having confidence even before you have it. That's how remarkable you are. You don't need to be confident before you start to FEEL confident. Today's lesson is all about identifying the feelings you will have when you are confident. Then, it's about evoking those feelings into your daily life.

How will you feel when you are confident? Will you be happy, fulfilled, at peace? Will you be more care-free? How will you know when you are confident?

Always remember that you must BE something before you see it in your life. If you want confidence, you must exude confidence. So, it is important for you to start identifying the feelings you will have when you are confident. Then, your job is to invite those feelings into your life.

Let's say that you envision yourself feeling happy and fulfilled when you are confident. How can you invite those feelings into your life? Well, you don't have to be confident first, before you invite happiness and fulfillment into your life. You can feel happy and fulfilled in so many other ways. You have access to these feelings, right now.

So think to yourself, what can you do today that makes you feel happy? That makes you fulfilled? Once you identify what that is for you, add that to your daily life!

When you start to feel happy and fulfilled, you invite confidence into your life. You start to feel how you envisioned yourself feeling. This in turn makes you feel confident. Do you see how this works? Invite the feelings you want to experience in your life, and then the manifestations will follow.

For today, I want you to start acting as if you are already confident. The way you think, feel, and carry yourself is very important. Think about the most confident version of yourself, how would she think? Act? Dress? Keep her home? Talk to herself? Be at work? Be with her friends?

You even may need to fake it until you make it, even if some days you may not be feeling your best! For example, some days I don't feel confident, but I engage in confident acts. I make sure to dress nice at work, even if I'm not feeling my best. I take care of myself. I make sure my hair looks nice. This helps me feel confident and it gets me out of my funk. If I were to go to work in my PJ's on that same day, I wouldn't be inviting the confident vibes in.

Day 18 Reflection

What feelings will you feel when you are THAT confident girl? List them all below.

How can you invite those feelings into your life today?

How can you start acting the part of the most confident you?

Is there anything in your environment that will be different once you are confident?

Commit to changing your environment in the way that will be different when you are confident. Detail a plan for how you can make this change.

Day 19: Kill The Comparison Habit

Day 19!! The lesson for Day 19 is all about stopping the one thing that kills your confidence the most, comparing yourself to others.

By constantly comparing ourselves to others, we dull our own shine. Comparing brings up a host of insecurities and doubts, for even the most confident people. This is why it's so important for you to understand how this habit can totally deter you from accomplishing your goals. It's time to drop the comparison habit, right now!

Our society love to compare. It seems like we are always looking at what others are doing, whether that's our friends, family members, celebrities or people we look up to. If you take one look at the media, it's all about celebrities and how much better they are doing than us. We see Kim Kardashian with her new Lamborghini or her 20 pound weight loss in 2 weeks. We see our favorite stars having the time of their lives vacationing in Hawaii.

Now with social media becoming so popular, we have easier access to compare ourselves to others. We deep down know that social media is not a true representation of someone's life, but we still compare ourselves to others on there. It's so much easier to feel insecure and doubtful about yourself when you are constantly looking at what others are doing. This social media habit can chip away at your confidence.

Do you know what the truth is? All of these celebrities with those beautiful pictures? It probably took 100 shots to get it. Just like when I take a selfie, it takes a good 10-20 to pick one! What others broadcast is what they are choosing to broadcast, remember this. As real as social media seems, it can be really fake.

Comparison can also be difficult to overcome because in some cultures, there's a heavy focus on comparison. Whether it's your family or friends focused on comparisons, or you find that most of your conversations focus on comparing others, it's a low vibe habit.

Comparison is downright dangerous to your self esteem and confidence. It robs you of YOU.

Here are some of the negative effects of comparison below.

1. Comparisons are unfair. We compare the worst we know about ourselves to the best of others.
2. Comparisons rob us of time spent focusing on what really matters, us! Minutes turn to hours as we compare with others.
3. We compare based on unrealistic standards.
4. Comparison robs you of your uniqueness, because you start to downplay yourself. You focus on what you aren't doing, instead of what you are doing.
5. Comparison puts focus on others, instead of yourself. Don't waste your precious energy focusing on others.

6. Comparison leads to resentment. We resent others for having something we think we don't have. It can ruin relationships.
7. Comparison leads to low self esteem and insecurity. The more we compare ourselves to others, the more insecure we get. We start to forget about all of the amazing qualities we have.
8. Comparison is extremely low vibe and low energy. In order to attract abundance into your life, you have to be in a good energy state. When you are in that low vibe state, you block positivity from finding you.
9. Comparison deprives us of happiness. We start to feel resentful, frustrated and insecure. That leaves us feeling frustrated.
10. Comparison takes us away from the present moment. By focusing on others, we lose the moment in front of us.
11. Comparison leads to low motivation. When we start to feel insecure about ourselves, our motivation decreases. We become disappointed that we aren't accomplishing what others are, so we lose the motivation to continue.

Do you see how dangerous and detrimental comparison is to our happiness, confidence, goals and joy? Comparison is the thief of joy.

I remember the days when I would compare my work to others. I would look at their pages and wish that my page looked like theirs. I would spend a lot of time on their websites, trying to find what they were doing to be successful and special. Before I knew it, I started to become frustrated and resentful. I began second guessing myself. I started to lose motivation.

By focusing so much on others, I lost sight of my own goals. I started to feel so frustrated that I decided that I would no longer look at other pages, unless I was briefly looking for some positivity or guidance. I started to focus on myself and my gifts.

I am now a much happier and confident person because of this practice. Most importantly, I started to notice that I had no reason to compare myself to others. I really had no idea what it took for others to get to where they are now.

Anytime you want to compare yourself to others, remind yourself that you really have no idea what that person did to get to where they are now. You really have no idea what their journey was like. Maybe their journey was filled with frustration, heartache and difficult times? No one becomes successful, confident or happy overnight.

We all go through a different journey, one that is not always advertised. So, remember to remind yourself that you don't know everyone's backstory and story to success.

For today's lesson, I want you to think about areas in your life where you find yourself comparing yourself to others. Really think deep about this, because releasing yourself from these comparisons can make a big difference for your confidence.

Once you realize that everyone is just like you, no matter who they are, you will feel better about yourself. Everyone has compared themselves to others at some point, the difference is that confident people have dropped this habit. Once you are confident with yourself, you won't have the need to compare yourself, as you realize that you are incomparable.

If others are comparing you to others, disengage from those conversations. Set boundaries. I know in some cultures it's common for comparisons, such as "Jill got her degree when she was 23, how come you are 25 and still haven't?", or "Mary is already married with kids, how come you are the same age and don't even have a boyfriend?". If you've ever been through this you know how difficult it can be.

My best guidance is to disengage. Don't give the comparisons attention. Wish the other party well and state that you don't believe in comparisons.

Everyone has their own journey and time for everything. I may get married at 30, while my best friend gets married at 25. There is nothing wrong with either of us! Just because it takes you longer to accomplish something, does not mean that there is something wrong with you.

Everything happens in divine timing. It's so important to realize where in your life you are holding yourself back by having unrealistic deadlines and standards. At times, a deadline is important, such as in work. In the other aspects of our life though, deadlines can become hindrances to accomplishing goals.

Our deadlines are based on norms and values from society. Who is society to tell us what our deadlines are? Why do we need to be married at a certain age, in college at a certain age and so forth? Are we living for ourselves or others? Is it more important to settle for marriage at 25 or be happily married at 30?

Make a pact to let go of deadlines to start living in the present moment, where the magic happens.

Day 19 Reflection

How has comparison harmed your confidence and life? How has it held you back?

What do you compare yourself to others about? List them below and be as specific as you can.

Are you ready to let go of the comparisons?

Today, I let go of comparing...

Write down how you will stop comparing yourself to others.
(Ex: I will stop checking up on social media religiously, I will disconnect from the phone more, etc)

Day 20:

Give Back To Others

Day 20 is all about giving back to others. Giving back to your community will help you feel fulfilled, happy and at peace.

Giving back means that you take the time to help others, give appreciation, or make an impact in some way. You can give back to the community, your family, friends, causes you enjoy and so forth. There is also no monetary value or pressure to give back in a grand way. Giving back is very simple and it's all about your intentions.

Giving back feels amazing. You will feel so good about yourself once you consistently give back to others. By spreading love to others, you give love to yourself. Some of the greatest joys in life come from giving back to others. When you help those around you, you invite that love back into your life.

Your biggest reward in giving back is the realization that you have made a positive and significant change in someone's life. That change is priceless.

Research has shown that giving back to others increases self esteem. Helping others helps us feel good about ourselves. There is something special about knowing that you have the power to help someone. The more you give back, the more you increase your self esteem and confidence.

Research also shows that volunteering increases physical health and personal empowerment in others. It's truly amazing what giving back can do for our well being. Not only do you improve your self love, you become happier and more fulfilled in life when you are able to make a difference.

Check out some of the other benefits of giving back below;

1. Fosters social connections - By giving back to others, we build social relationships. We interact with others with similar values and interests. This helps foster a greater send of camaraderie.

2. Helps the community - Doing something for your community helps all those around you. By helping your community, you help yourself. You also can inspire others to do the same.

3. Allows you to gain a new perspective - We often are so focused on our lives, we forget that there are billions of people to connect with. My connecting with others and hearing their stories, we get offered a new perspective. Often, we don't realize how good we have it, until we meet someone who is struggling more than us.

4. Helps you feel needed - We humans want to feel needed and appreciated. It's one of our basic human needs. When you give back, you are meeting this need of yours, which fulfills you on a deep level.

5. Helps change the world - People like you are needed to change the world. If we all give back and dedicate our time to positivity, more positivity will follow in this world. By giving

back you set a good example and inspire others to give back as well.

There are so many benefits of giving back, all of which are important in their own right. For today, I want you to focus on what you can do for your community, family, friends & environment.

Day 20 Reflection

What is one thing you can do today or in the near future to give back?

Are there any causes/communities/groups that you are passionate about helping?

How can you be more of service to your family, friends, community?

How can you add "giving back" into your schedule?

How do you feel knowing that you have the potential to change lives?

Day 21: Reflect

WOW! Day 21 at last. I can't believe that this is the last day of this wonderful journey. I am so excited you have reach the last day. These 3 weeks have been difficult, tough, and challenging, but you did it!

I am so happy for you that you have completed this journey. I hope that you have learned valuable lessons that you can take with you throughout your whole life. My hope is that you consistently apply this material into your life. It's impossible to do everything all at once, but adding these positive habits into your life will tremendously improve your quality of loving.

Your confidence is a work in progress. At this point, I hope that you feel an increase in your confidence. You may be feeling lighter, happier and more at peace. These are all signs of increased confidence! If you feel better about yourself, than you have done the work. Continue to make yourself a priority and do the work as needed.

Confidence is a journey. It's best to practice these principles as much as you can. You can also go through this guide as many times as you want.

You have done the inner work necessary for confidence. You have all of the control in your life. No matter what it is that you want to accomplish, such as self love, a relationship, a business and so forth, you have all the power. Once you do the inner work, everything else will easily come to you.

By deciding to work on your confidence, you have decided that you are important and worthy of your love.

For today, I want you to reflect upon all the work you have done, as well as the work you need to continue doing. Remember, this is all a journey. Where you are now is not where you were before, which is amazing progress in its own right. Continue on with these practices, and in a few months you will be amazed at all the progress you have made.

I love you and I thank you for being here on this journey. Here is to you!

Take a look at the goals and questions you answered on Day 1. Then come back here and write your answers below accordingly.

Day 21 Reflection

Were you able to accomplish any of your confidence goals? Which ones?

Which goals do you still need to work on?

Do you feel more confident now? How do you know that you are? What positive feelings do you feel?

Which daily lessons helped you improve your confidence the most?

Which lessons do you still need more practice in?

How has this 21 day journey been for you?

What have you learned about yourself on this journey?

How will you continue to work on your confidence and self love after today?

About the Author

Jacqueline Kademian is a Licensed Marriage & Family Therapist, Author and Entrepreneur. She is the creator of the personal development brand, Positive Soul. She uses spirituality and psychology techniques to help others create massive changes in their lives. Specializing in relationships, self-love, mindset and manifestation work, she is able to help her clients' create lasting change. Jacqueline is unique with her soft-spoken, clear, and relatable teaching style. She is able to provide healing and transformation by helping her clients' find their power and greatness.

If you'd like to find out more about Jacqueline and the other products she offers, visit her on her website, https://positivesoul.net. You can also find her on Instagram, @positive___soul, where she posts inspirational content.

Listen to her podcast on iTunes, by searching for "Positive Soul Podcast".

Made in the USA
Las Vegas, NV
15 January 2024

84410897R00109